CONTENTS

ISBN 978-0-7935-5669-4

G. SCHIRMER, Inc.

DISTRIBUTED BY
HAL•LEONARD® CORPORATION
7777 W. BLUEMOUND RD. P.O. BOX 13819 MILWAUKEE, WI 53213

First Instruction in Piano-playing.

One hundred Recreations.

CARL CZERNY.

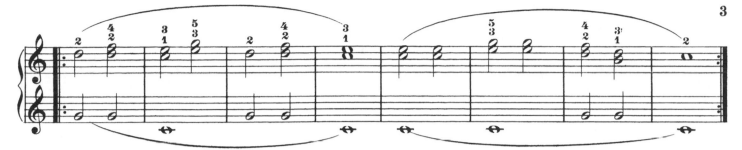

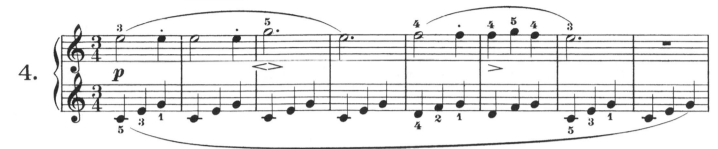

4.

5.

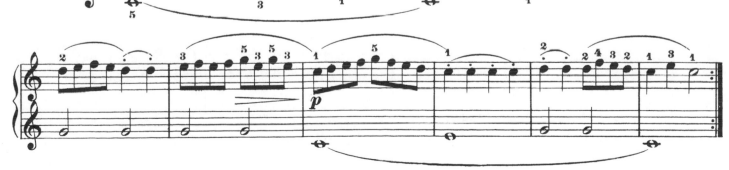

4

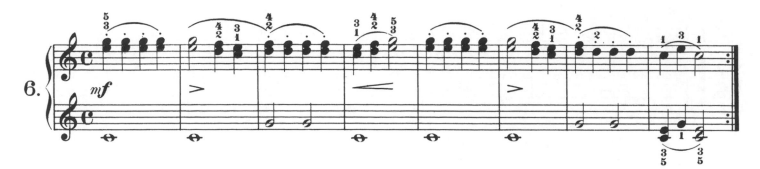

6.

Bohemian Air.
Andante.

7.

Allegretto.

8.

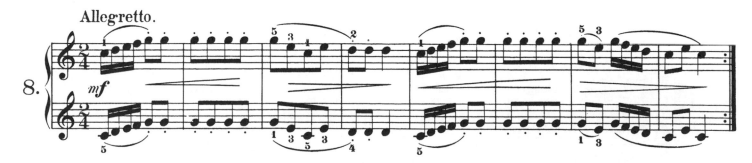

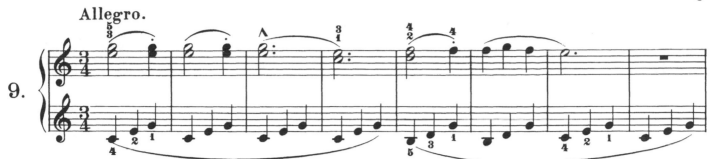

9.

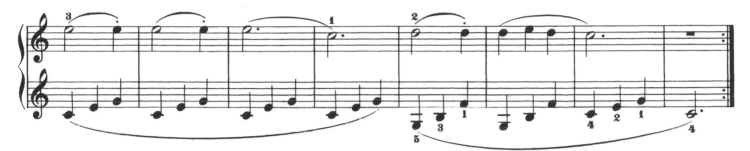

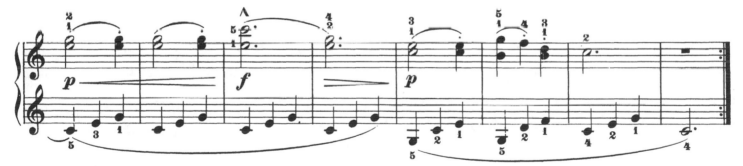

10.

Allegro.

11.

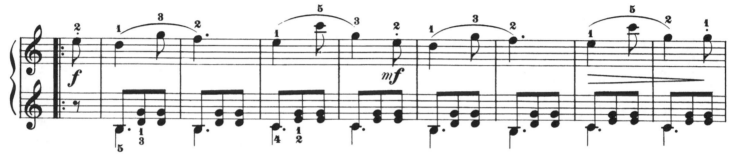

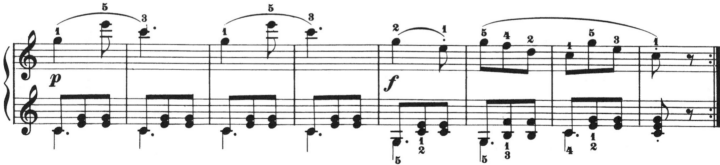

Allegretto.

12.

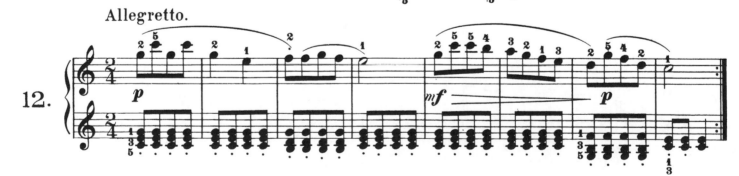

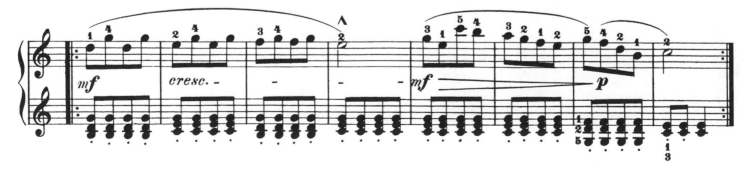

Allegretto

13.

Austrian Waltz.
Allegretto

14.

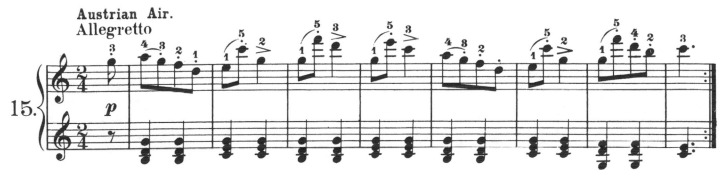

Austrian Air.
Allegretto

15.

8

Waltz on a French Romance.
Allegretto.

16.

Gavotte.
Allegro.

17.

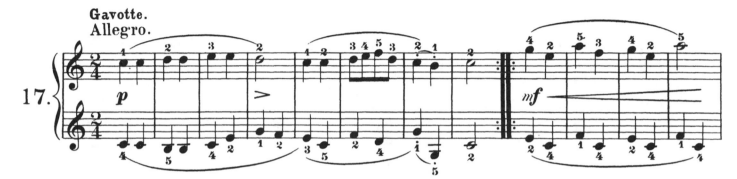

Italian Theme.
Allegro.

18.

19. Allegro.

10

Marlborough.
Allegretto.

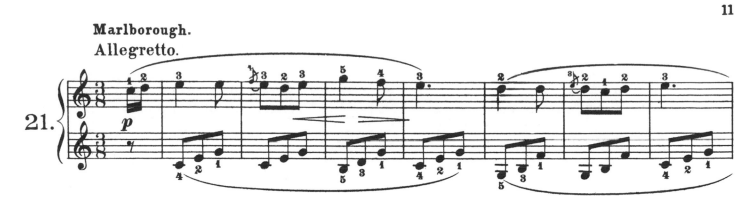

21.

French Air.
Allegretto.

22.

12

Austrian Theme.
Allegretto.

25.

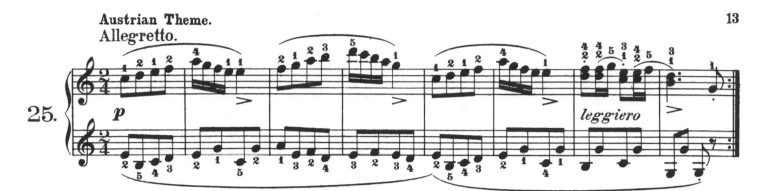

English Theme.
Allegretto moderato.

26.

14

Bohemian Song.
Allegro moderato.

27.

Allegro.

28.

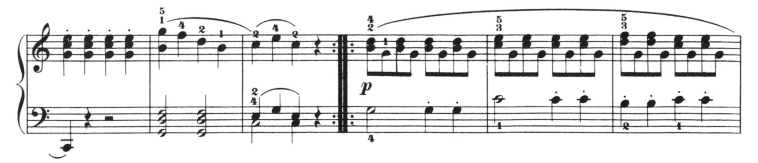

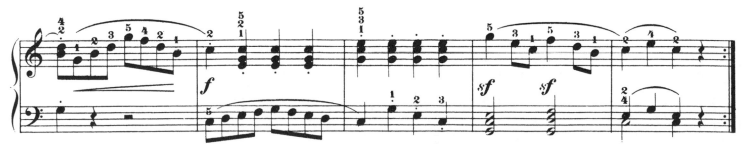

Prelude.

Allegro moderato.

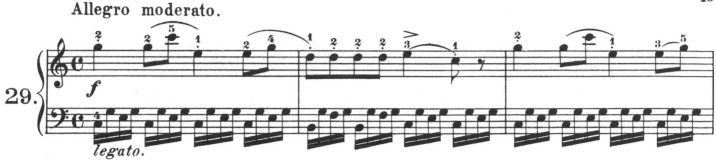

29.

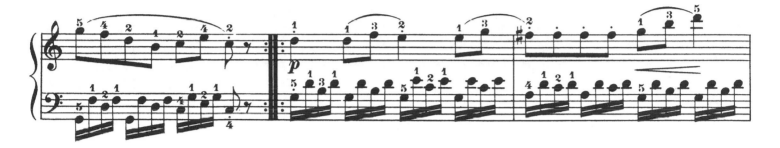

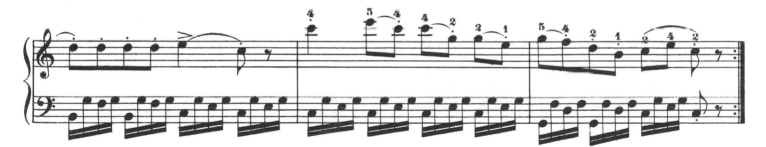

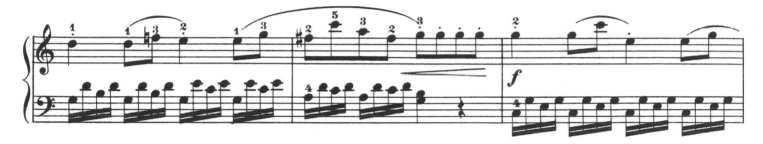

Allegro.

30.

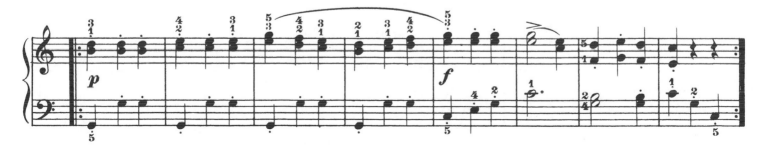

Russian Theme.
Allegretto.

31.

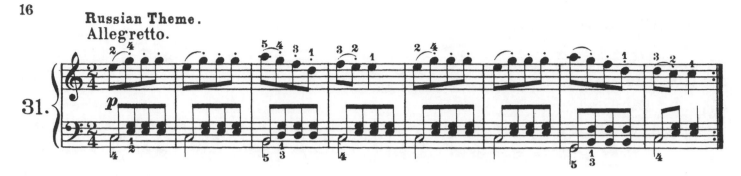

German Air.
Allegretto.

32.

Allegretto vivace.

33.

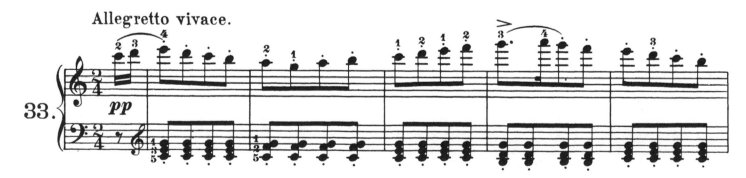

French Romance: "Ma Fanchette est charmante."
Allegretto.

Prelude.

Alexander March.
Allegro.

35.

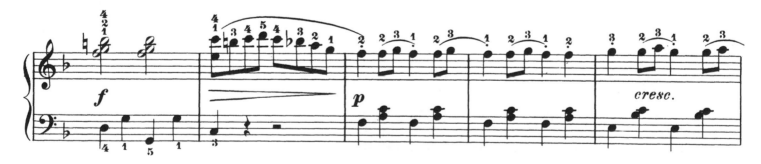

Swiss Air.
Allegrètto moderato.

36.

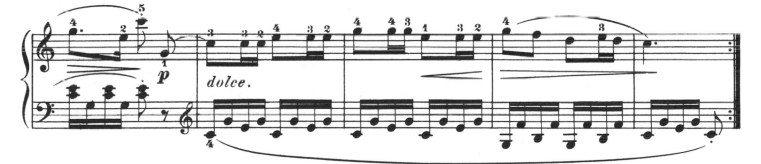

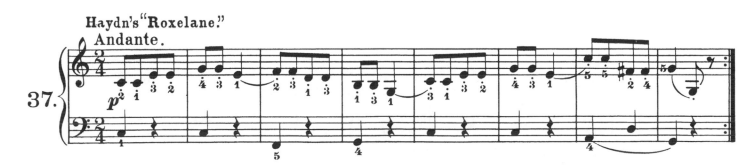

Haydn's "Roxelane."
Andante.

37.

20

Romance from "Fra Diavolo."
Allegretto moderato.

38.

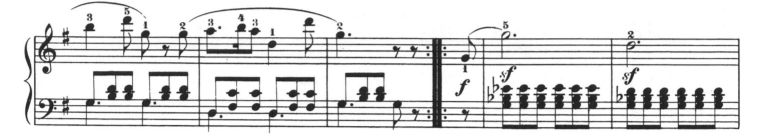

Tyrolienne.
Allegretto.

39.

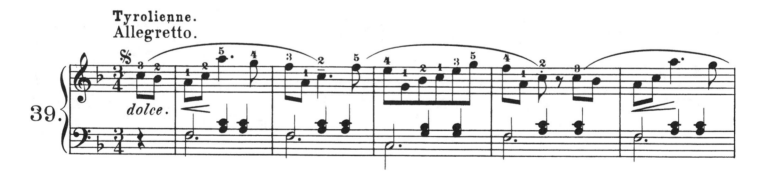

Fine.

Da Capo.

Italian theme.
Andantino grazioso.

40.

Theme by Mozart.
Allegretto.

41.

Theme by Weigl.
Allegretto.

42.

Theme by Weigl.
Allegro moderato.

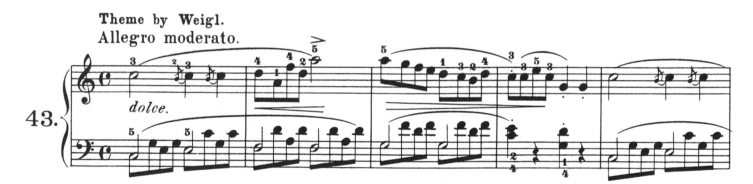

43.

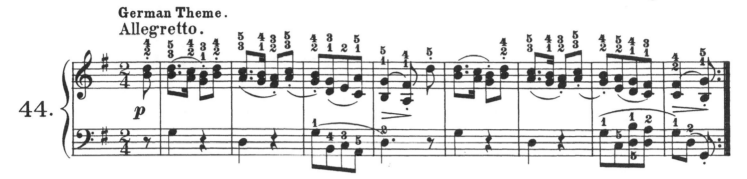

Tyrolese Air.
Allegretto.

46.

Theme by Gluck.
Allegretto.

47.

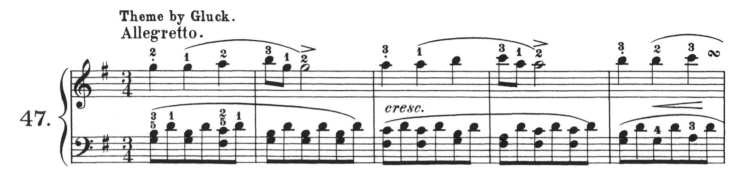

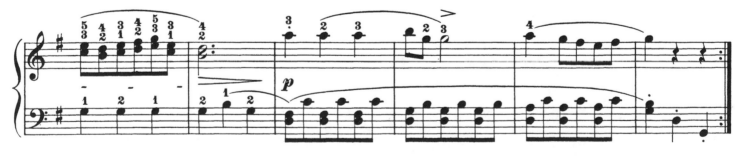

Russian Theme.
Allegretto moderato.

48.

Tyrolese Air.
Allegretto.

49.

Scotch Air.
Allegretto moderato.

50.

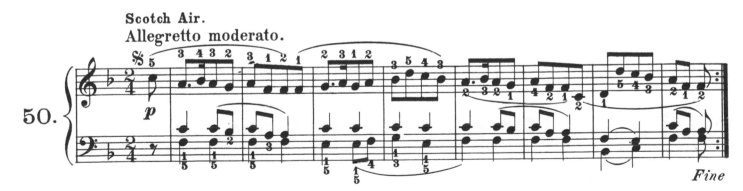

Fine

Da Capo

English Air.
Allegretto.

51.

March by Meyerbeer.
Allegro moderato.

52.

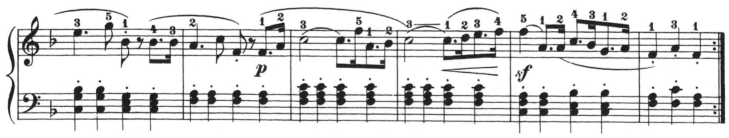

Scotch Air.
Allegro moderato.

53.

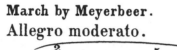

"La belle Cathérine."
Allegretto.

54.

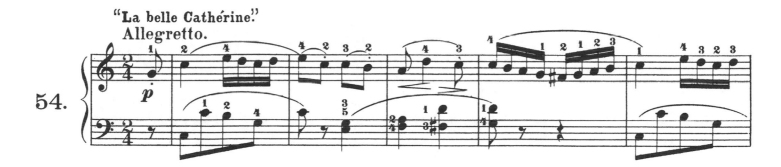

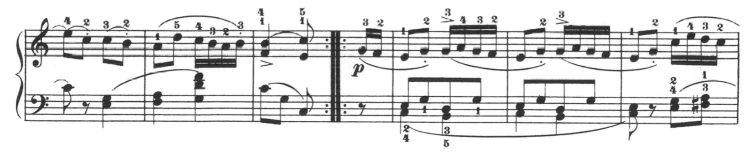

French Air.
Andantino.

55.

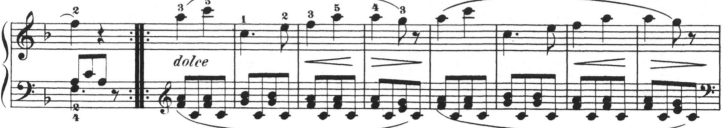

Waltz, by Mozart.
Allegro.

56.

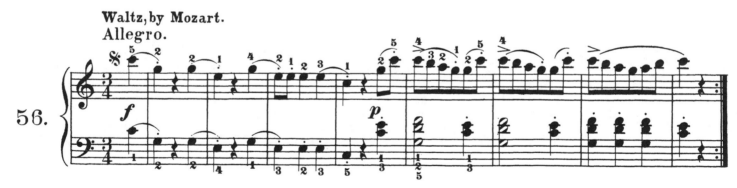

Fine

Trio.

legato

Valse D.C. al Fine

Italian Air: "Vien quà, Dorina bella."
Allegretto grazioso.

57.

Theme from "The Pirate", by Bellini.
Moderato.

58.

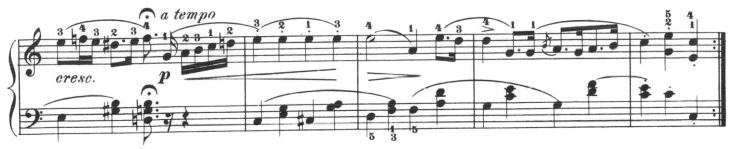

French Air: "Au clair de la lune."
Allegretto vivo.

59.

Theme by C. Czerny.
Allegretto moderato.

60.

Scotch Air.
Allegretto moderato.

61.

Italian Air. "Sul margine d'un rio."
Allegretto moderato.

62.

Theme from "Alceste," by Weigl.
Allegro moderato.

63.

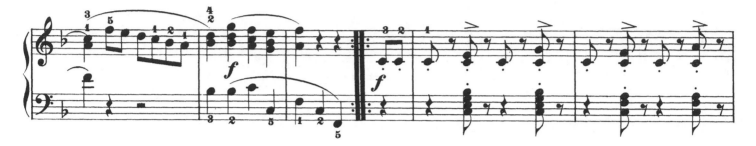

Tyrolese Air.
Allegretto moderato.

64.

Scotch Air.
Allegretto.

65.

Theme from "La Straniera," by Bellini.
Andantino.

66.

34

Italian Air. "Nel cor più non mi sento."
Andantino.

67.

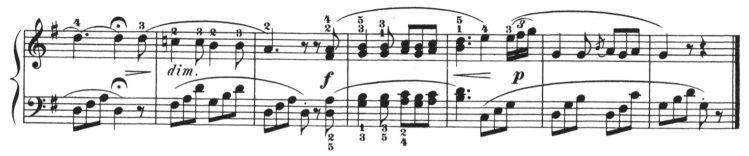

Air de Ballet.
Allegretto.

68.

Prelude.

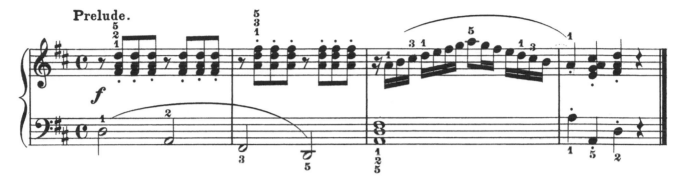

Hunters' Chorus from "Der Freischütz", by Weber.
Allegretto.

69.

Italian Theme from "La Straniera," by Bellini.

Allegro moderato.

70.

Swiss Air.

Allegretto moderato.

71.

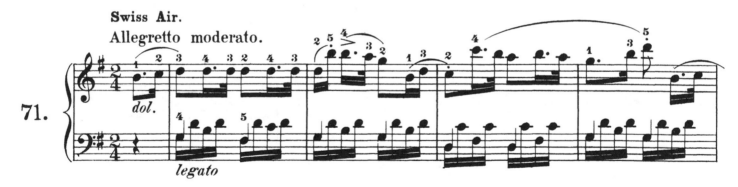

Waltz, by Hummel.
Allegro vivace.

Waltz, by Count Gallenberg.
Allegretto moderato.

38

Waltz, by Weber.
Allegretto moderato.

74.

Swiss Air.
Allegretto.

75.

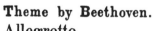

Theme by Beethoven.
Allegretto.

76.

Theme from "l'Elisire d'Amore," by Donizetti.
Allegretto

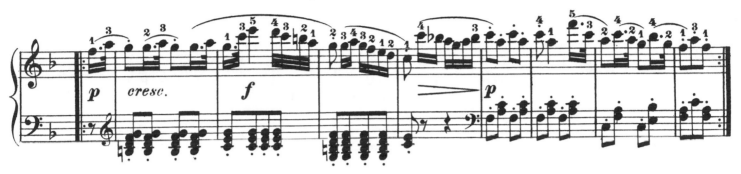

Theme from "La Cenerentola," by Rossini.
Allegro moderato

40

Italian Canzonet.
Allegretto.

79.

From "Preciosa," by Weber.
Andantino.

80.

German Air.
Andante espressivo.

81.

Scotch Air.
Allegro.

French Romance. "Partant pour la Syrie."
Allegretto.

83.

Prelude.

Theme by Weber.
Andante.

84.

Fine.

Da Capo al Fine.

From "Don Giovanni," by Mozart.
Allegretto moderato.

85.

poco cresc.

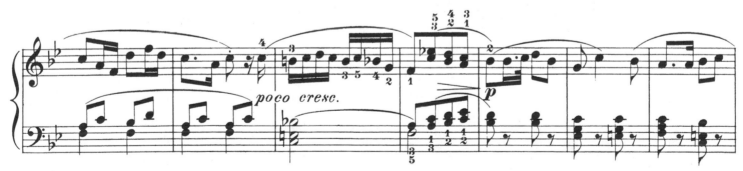

Theme by Paganini.
Allegretto.

86.

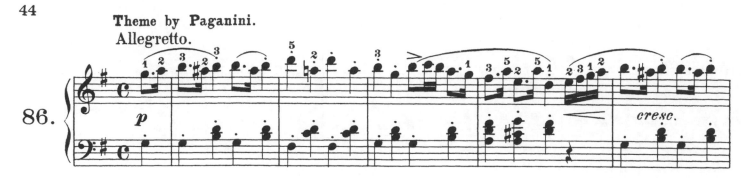

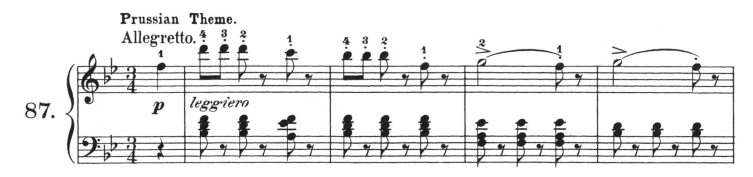

Prussian Theme.
Allegretto.

87.

Theme from "Norma," by Bellini.
Allegretto.

88.

legato

Scotch Air.
Allegro.

89.

Theme from "Anna Bolena," by Donizetti.
Allegretto moderato.

90.

Italian Theme, by Pacini.
Allegro.

91.

Theme from "Zampa" by Hérold.
Allegretto.

92.

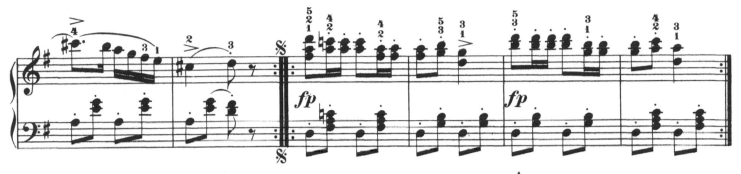

Scotch Air.
Allegretto.

93.

Theme, by Haydn.
Andante.

94.

English National Air.
Andante.

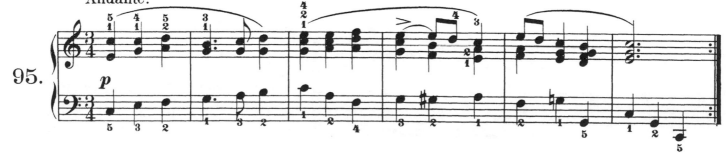

95.

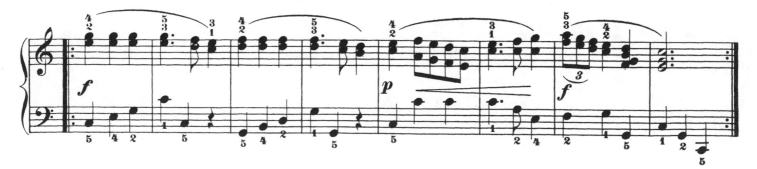

Russian National Air.
Allegro.

96.

German Air, by Himmel.
Andantino grazioso.

97.

Rule Britannia; English Air.
Allegretto.

98.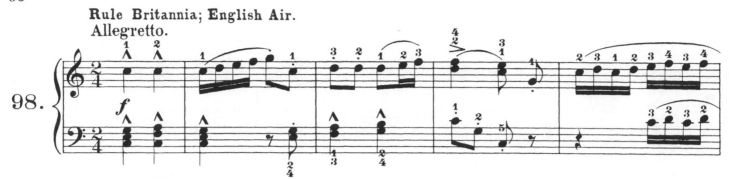

German Arietta.
Allegretto.

99.

Polonaise.
Allegretto.

100.

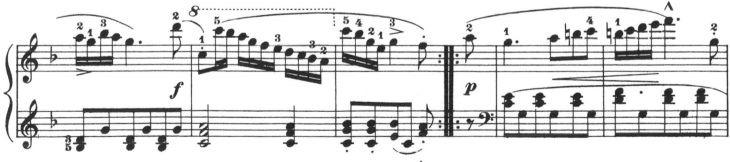